LEADER GUIDE

WHERE DO BROKEN HEARTS GO?

HEALING AND HOPE
AFTER ABORTION

JANE ABBATE

**Messy
Miracles
Books**

Where Do Broken Hearts Go? Leader Guide

Copyright © 2014 Jane Abbate

Published by Messy Miracles, PO Box 22, Wildwood, PA 15091-1001.

Disclaimer: This book is intended for general education purposes only. It is not intended as a substitute for therapy, as a "self-help" guide, or as a training manual for therapists interested in post-abortion counseling. If expert assistance or counseling is needed, the services of a competent professional should be sought.

ISBN-13: 978-0-9828486-1-6

Printed in the United States of America on acid-free paper.
Editor: Pamela Guerrieri, proofedtoperfection.com

Cover and Book Design: Patricia Bacall, bacallcreative.com

Attention Pregnancy Resource Centers, Non-Profit Organizations, Churches, Colleges, Universities, and Professional Organizations: Quantity discounts are available on bulk purchases of this book for educational training, fund raising, or gift-giving. For more information contact Messy Miracles, PO Box 22, Wildwood, PA 15091-1001.

NOTE TO READERS:

For simplicity, the author has used the feminine pronouns, she, her, hers, herself, throughout this Leader Guide in reference to both leaders and participants involved in post abortion healing. The author fully acknowledges that both women and men can serve as excellent leaders of post abortion healing. Further, the author acknowledges that both women and men experience heartbreak following abortion and may find support through the Where Do Broken Hearts Go? resources for post abortion healing.

Also for clarification, the following abbreviations are used throughout this book to reference companion books written by the author:

Where Do Broken Hearts Go?: WDBHG
Where Do Broken Hearts Go? Leader Guide: WDBHG Leader Guide
Where Do Broken Hearts Go? Study Journal: WDBHG Study Journal

Copies of all forms are available for download from the Messy Miracles website: messymiracles.com.

This book is dedicated to the leaders, staff, and volunteers
of the Women's Choice Network
who reach out with compassion and wisdom—
no matter what.

"By their fruit you will recognize them."

Matthew 7:20

IN APPRECIATION FOR:

Bill Abbate: Your support and love for me are endless. Next to my salvation, I treasure you the most.

Cheryl Ryan: The Light of Life exercise is all from you and I appreciate your permission to share this gem of inspiration and hope with my readers. God bless you!

Pamela: Thank you for trusting me and agreeing to co-lead in the very first WDBHG support group. Your thoughtful and loving wisdom made all the difference in the content of this material. You are my sister in Christ and I love and appreciate you!

About the Author

Jane Abbate knows about abortion and how it changes a life forever. Through firsthand experience with her own abortions, and through her years of work with women as a Rachel's Vineyard retreat team volunteer, she has built a solid foundation for helping others deal with their experience of abortion. She lives the healing process she teaches: Face the past, mourn the losses, turn, and draw closer to God.

Jane is the founder of Messy Miracles, a ministry which helps people who struggle with guilt, shame and regret. Her training as a certified coach, and extensive experience guiding people in behavior change, make Jane the ideal person to help others face their "messy" lives and move forward with hope.

Jane is the author of *Where Do Broken Hearts Go?* and the companion resources, *Where Do Broken Hearts Go? Leader Guide* and *Where Do Broken Hearts Go? Study Journal.*

Jane lives in Pittsburgh, PA with her husband, Bill, and is an active member of her church.

She is a popular speaker and is available for speaking engagements and group leader training. She can be contacted through her website messymiracles.com, by email to jane@messymiracles.com or by writing to:

Jane Abbate
Messy Miracles
PO Box 22, Wildwood, PA 15091-1001

TABLE OF CONTENTS

PART I

PLANNING AND PREPARATION

WELCOME!

What great joy it is to connect with you, dear faithful one of God and messenger of hope! You are taking on an amazing leadership role as you step out into this healing ministry for the victims of abortion. God has so much in store for you and the people you will serve.

I wrote *Where Do Broken Hearts Go?* to provide a compassionate and private way for women to explore their experience of abortion. This is not an easy subject to talk about, and many people bury their emotions for a long time. But remaining numb or refusing to examine the grief and loss that follow abortion only prevent us from healing. More importantly, we miss out on the powerful miracles God has in store for us.

It has been so gratifying to hear how my own journey toward healing resonates with women from all walks of life, all over the world, and how they no longer feel alone. The feedback of how women have either strengthened their relationship with our Lord and Savior, Jesus Christ, or finally found their way to Him for the first time has been even more precious to me.

Shortly after publication, the leaders of the Women's Choice Network (mypregnancycenter.org) in Pittsburgh, Pennsylvania, invited me to train and mentor staff and volunteers to run support groups for post-abortive women, using my book as a guide. They sought a resource that was grounded in Holy Scripture but would not be overwhelming, as many of their clients are not familiar with God's Word. They were also sensitive to the limited time that clients would realistically commit to a group. We began our first support group in 2011.

Although participants were initially reluctant to open up to strangers, the atmosphere of love and support created by the group leaders calmed fears and encouraged sharing. So many women said, *"I thought I was the only one. I can't believe that anyone else could understand how I felt."* There were real breakthroughs when secrets were revealed yet the participants were met with acceptance and compassion. Encouraged by these results, the Women's Choice Network is now using *Where Do Broken Hearts Go?* as their preferred resource for post-abortion counseling and education.

The *Where Do Broken Hearts Go? Leader Guide* was written to support the dedicated and loving women who lead these support groups. It connects the 19 emotions covered in *Where Do Broken Hearts Go?* and builds on the Reflection Exercises included in each chapter of the book. In the following pages there is a wealth of resources to help you setup, publicize and lead six, one-on-one or small group sessions. All of the handouts for each session are included and may be reproduced for distribution to your group participants. In addition, the *Where Do Broken Hearts Go? Study Journal* is available for purchase for those participants who desire a complete copy of all of the material covered in the sessions.

My goal is to provide as much support as possible for leaders who offer support and hope to those who struggle with abortion. I welcome feedback and invite you to contact me if I can support you and your team in any way.

A Prayer for Leaders

Father God,

My dear sister in Christ is beginning holy work. You, Father, have appointed her to reach out to women who have experienced abortion, to minister to those whose hearts are broken. Romans 8:28 promises that in all things God works for the good of those who love Him, who have been called according to His purpose. I pray for Your blessing over every aspect of this work.

Prepare this leader's heart. Clothe her with mercy, kindness, and gentleness (Col 3:12) as the stories of suffering unfold. Give her confidence, Lord, relying on the power of the Holy Spirit (1 Cor 2:4) and not just her own knowledge or experience. Increase her patience, remembering how You wait for all of us to turn to You to be saved (2 Pet 3:15). Remind her to be humble, acknowledging that we are all sinners, saved only by Your grace (Phil 2:3).

This woman has a dream of doing something for You. Do not allow the enemy to discourage or confuse her. Father, You are Sovereign—in control of all things and ruler over all things. There is absolutely nothing that happens in the universe that is outside of Your influence and authority. May she feel Your presence and protection at every moment.

I claim Your blessings upon this woman as she begins this challenging yet rewarding ministry. Bring energy and encouragement at just the right moment when obstacles threaten to derail her efforts. Provide the people and resources she needs to complete this work. May the time and effort she devotes to the healing of those who suffer from abortion be fully pleasing in Your sight. May she reap eternal rewards for herself and for those You want her to serve.

In the name of Jesus, Your Son, and our beloved Savior, I pray. Amen.

Jane Abbate, Author

PURPOSE OF THE SUPPORT GROUP

Abortion is a deeply personal experience that has a tremendous emotional impact, whether a woman realizes it or not. The purpose of this group is to support women to move beyond numbness, denial, and shame and take a realistic look at how abortion has affected her life.

Emotions are a gift from God. They are normal, not symptoms of disease or weakness. Emotions provide clues about what we are thinking and feeling, and they often drive our behavior. It is the hiding, denying, and burying of emotions that get people in trouble. Think of emotions as energy. When we are not willing or able to allow that energy to flow freely, the energy can get stuck in our bodies and create all kinds of physical issues and illness. We can also make impetuous, poor choices or say and do things that hurt the people we love when we are not aware of what we are feeling or when we allow our emotions to take over.

Abortion can be such a difficult experience that a woman is afraid to acknowledge how she feels about it. She is afraid she will become overwhelmed. It is true that as she reflects on how abortion has impacted her and her unborn child's life, troubling emotions such as guilt, anger, or fear may rise up. However, as she learns to face whatever she is feeling, the energy of these difficult emotions becomes a new resource that she can embrace to generate new strength, expanded possibilities, and stronger muscle for change. There is new meaning in what had been a difficult experience. Now, the woman can feel empowered to make conscious and intentional choices to create the fulfilling life God has planned for her.

THE QUALIFICATIONS OF A LEADER

Not everyone who steps forward with a desire to lead a post-abortion support group is ready or capable to take on this important responsibility. Group leaders must be prepared to carry out their roles with clarity, competence, and confidence. Listed below are several important qualifications of a successful group leader.

MATURE CHRISTIAN

What happens when a group member is convicted of sin during the discussion and begins weeping? Who can readily pronounce God's Word through Scripture to combat an attack by the enemy? Who calls the group to prayer when a group member confesses to being on the brink of divorce? These situations require a leader who can take control and help the group follow the Holy Spirit. In considering the qualifications of a group leader, ask:

- What is your personal testimony of faith?
- Are you an active member of a church or faith community? Can you provide a reference from a member of the pastoral staff?
- Describe your prayer life and your own spiritual disciplines, e.g., Bible study, small group participation, etc.

LEADER

Group leaders need to do just that—lead. Your job is to create an environment that allows group members to explore their personal experience with abortion and to connect with the healing power of the Holy Spirit. Effective group leaders possess various skills and apply key practices to be used during group meetings, including facilitating effective discussion, understanding different learning and personality styles, interpreting body language, handling conflict, incorporating worship, and so on. In considering the qualifications of a group leader, ask:

- What is your goal for leading this support group? How did you come to be called to this work?

- What are your experiences leading small groups?
- Tell me about a time when you had to handle a difficult situation with a group member. What were the circumstances, how did you handle it, and what was the result?

PERSONAL HEALING EXPERIENCE

It is valuable and preferable for a member of the leadership team to have personal experience with abortion. This creates a sense of trust and empathy among the participants. But not all women who have had abortions will make good group leaders. In considering the qualifications of a group leader, ask:

- What is your personal experience with abortion? What healing work have you done, e.g. Forgiven and Set Free Bible Study, Rachel's Vineyard, Surrendering the Secret? What has been the impact?

- How would you describe where you are now in your personal healing journey? How do you hope that leading this support group will influence your own healing?

- What is your relationship with your aborted child? Have you named him/her?

- If you have not experienced abortion, in what ways have you aborted God's will for your life? Is there another area of sin for which you have unresolved grief, feelings of unforgiveness, or that troubles you? What has been your healing experience?

TIME AND ENERGY

Starting up and leading a support group takes time and energy. Recruiting and orienting new members, preparing for each session, leading the sessions, and supporting members between meetings are just a few important responsibilities. In considering the qualifications of a group leader, ask:

- How much time do you expect to devote to all the aspects of leading this group?

- How will you make time for this work in your schedule? What time constraints or limitations will you be working under, e.g., may have to work last-minute overtime, take care of children, etc.?

NOTES

NOTES

THE ROLE OF A LEADER

There will be many tasks and responsibilities that a group leader will handle during the course of running a *Where Do Broken Hearts Go?* support group. Some of the most critical are described below:

PRAY

The founders of smallgroupsbigimpact.com found that, overwhelmingly, healthy small groups have group leaders who pray for their group participants every day. And that makes sense when you understand that it is the Holy Spirit who is responsible for our spiritual growth and emotional development. So if you want to support them, spend time in prayer, asking the Holy Spirit to give you compassion, wisdom, clarity, and power. Trust Him to guide and protect you, as He works through you to change lives. He will not let you down!

SCREEN AND ORIENT PARTICIPANTS

It is an act of courage for a woman to reach out and seek help for healing from abortion. Your first contact is an opportunity to demonstrate the compassion and support that will be available to her in your group. It is important for the group leader to spend about 30 to 60 minutes with each participant, ideally in person, in advance of the first meeting. The *Participant Information Form* has been provided to guide your discussion, but do not allow it to get in the way of establishing a relationship with this woman. It is also important to provide details about the group and to answer questions. Not everyone is ready or willing to do the work involved in this study. So this is a time for you both to explore whether this is a good fit.

The *Participant Information Form* can be used to guide your conversation and to record notes. It includes an overview of what is involved in the study that should be reviewed with each participant. You are not looking to learn all the details of her background. In fact, to do so would probably be overwhelming and offensive. Use your best judgment as to how much asking, listening, and explaining is best in this first contact. Keep in mind how sensitive and difficult this conversation will be for the woman, so do all you can to demonstrate that you are trustworthy and compassionate.

PREPARE

As you prepare to lead this support group, carefully and prayerfully read *WDBHG*. Make notes; highlight key sections, stories, or quotes; and complete the Reflection Exercises at the end of each chapter. Be sure to allow time in your schedule to look over the material prior to each session. If you are working with a partner, it is helpful to discuss in advance who might introduce each topic. However, being flexible and responding in the moment to who is leading the discussion is also important. Before each session begins, dedicate time to pray, asking the Holy Spirit to calm, center you and unite you with your partner.

LEAD THE GROUP DISCUSSION

The detailed session outlines that are provided contain the recommended topics, activities and questions for each meeting. Because it is important to allow ample time for sharing among participants, you may find that there is more material included than you will likely have time to cover. This *WDBHG Leader Guide* also includes tips on handling difficult situations so take a few minutes and read through those suggestions and consider how you might handle these challenges. While you should not dominate the discussion, if you have personal experience with abortion, feel free to add your own story to illustrate a particular point. Participants may find it helpful and encouraging to hear how you have healed and moved on from difficult emotions. If you have not personally experienced abortion, reflect on another way you have aborted God's will for your life so that you can identify and empathize with the participants and occasionally share your own emotional pain.

OFFER COMPASSION, WITHHOLD JUDGMENT OR ADVICE

You will be guiding women to see their abortion experience in a new light. Each participant will have her own unique story and experience. While there may be similarities among participants or to your own life, keep in mind that there is no right way to grieve or process an abortion. Trust that the Holy Spirit will reveal what is important to each woman. If you are new to leading support groups or to abortion healing, it may be beneficial to refer women with particularly difficult backgrounds to abortion-specific healing ministries such as Rachel's Vineyard (rachelsvineyard.org).

Your role is to ask thoughtful questions, guide discussions, and provide a safe and prayerful atmosphere for reflection and sharing. If asked for advice or if you find yourself dealing with a situation beyond your capabilities, be candid and simply say, *That's not something I am comfortable with or prepared to address. Let's talk about where you can get the answer.* Group leaders are encouraged to have the names and contact information for local qualified Christian counselors, especially those experienced with post-traumatic stress disorders (PTSD) or post-abortion trauma, in case a referral would be useful.

LET GO AND LET GOD

You cannot force your group members to grow spiritually any more than you can force them to grow taller. No matter how good you become at facilitating discussion, creating awareness, leading prayer, or handling difficult situations, participants will not become healed unless they are led by the Holy Spirit. Do your best and leave the rest to Him, remembering, "He is God and I am not!"

NOTES

NOTES

LEADING THE GROUP

OVERVIEW

The *WDBHG Leader Guide* has been prepared to help you plan and lead a group of women who desire emotional and spiritual healing following abortion. It provides content for six confidential, nonjudgmental, and Holy Spirit-filled group sessions. The format was designed for 90-minute sessions, but you can adjust the number and duration of the sessions to fit the size and needs of the group. The ideal group size is four to eight women so that participants have ample time to share their experiences and emotions. Although this six-week format can be used for meeting on a one-on-one basis, a woman is often best served in a group where sharing and support can occur without singular focus on herself.

In Session One, participants will introduce themselves and commit to the ground rules of the group. Another important goal of this session is for the participants to tell the story of their abortion(s). Throughout the remaining five weeks, details will emerge, so in this first session, the priority is to allow each woman to express her experience as best she can at that time. The handout *Sharing My Abortion Story* can be distributed to help guide the participants through this often painful process.

The remaining five sessions explore a variety of emotions often experienced before, during, and after abortion. Each week, there are reading assignments in *WDBHG* and participants are encouraged to complete the Reflection Exercises at the end of each chapter. Participants may also choose to purchase the *WDBHG Study Journal,* which follows the same six-week format as the *WDBHG Leader Guide*. This optional material will enable them to follow along more closely with the content of each session and provides space to reflect and record their most valuable take-aways.

Each group session allocates time for individual reflection, group discussion, and interactive activities so that the participants gain additional insights and deeper understanding of their abortion experience. Participants often draw closer to one another as they share their thoughts, personal experiences, needs, concerns, and hopes for the future.

Although there is truth to the saying, "The more you put into it the more you'll get out of it," in today's busy, jammed-packed world, it is unrealistic to count on all participants to complete all of the preparation for each session. So, meet the participants where they are and be confident that their regular attendance at the group sessions is evidence of their intention to find healing from abortion.

GENERAL TIPS

- Provide copies of *WDBHG* and *WDBHG Study Journal* for purchase either in advance of or at the first session. If possible, make scholarship available for those who cannot afford the materials.

- Create a comfortable and private environment for the group. Arrange chairs in a circle. Provide nametags for at least the first few sessions.

- You may choose to serve a light snack and/or beverage, but it is not necessary. Keep in mind that some participants may be struggling with food allergies, restrictions, or addictions, so it is best to keep refreshments simple and healthy. One exception is the final session when you may choose to create a celebration to mark the end of their hard work and God's blessings. However, always make sure you provide healthy options.

- Offer to prepare and distribute a sign-in sheet with names, e-mail addresses, and phone numbers so that members can keep in touch after the group ends. Make it clear that disclosure of contact information is entirely optional. Some participants may prefer to protect their privacy.

- Have a Bible, plenty of tissues, extra pens, pencils, and paper available for each session.

- Time is precious to everyone and it is important to be a good time-keeper. Start and end each session on time. It is unfair to those who are punctual to be kept waiting for latecomers. This is particularly important in the first session when anxiety is very high. Respect that some participants might be on a tight schedule and may not be able to stay late. Allow about ten minutes to wrap up each session and be sure to close each session with prayer. Everyone needs the benefit of a proper closing and not to feel they have missed something.

- Very personal details will be shared in these sessions. Distribute the *Accountability Covenant* and make sure that you stress the ground rules for privacy and confidentiality. Asking the participants to sign and return a copy of this document reinforces the importance of creating a safe environment for everyone, inside and outside of the group sessions. Read the expectations out loud and ask participants to indicate agreement by raising their hands.

- Tailor the amount of content to the time allowed. Each session outline includes more questions than time will likely allow, so don't feel pressured to cover everything. Pick one or two questions that relate most to the group members and focus on those. Allowing silence is a good thing, as providing time to process and reflect is an important part of healing. So, be patient and don't rush to fill the silence with your own response or another question.

- At some point, usually at the start of each session, allow time for participants to ask questions about the reading assignment or to share their responses to the Reflection Exercises. There will not be time to cover all of the homework, so ask participants to choose what meant the most to them that week from the homework.

TIPS ON HANDLING DIFFICULTIES IN THE GROUP

By covering the details in the *Accountability Covenant*, leaders can prepare participants for what is expected of them in the group. Take the time to review this document, considering the points below:

- The focus of the support group is abortion recovery. Even though participants may have other hurts and emotional damage, it is important to keep the primary focus of the group on the abortion experience. Gently redirect discussion if it wanders and other troubling situations such as divorce, rape, sexual abuse, financial or family member problems begin to take over. You, as the leader, can offer support by saying,

I realize that this is very important to you. Since the focus of this group is abortion healing, can we meet afterward and discuss how you can get the support you need?

- Keep in mind that people are different. Some think out loud; others need time to process their thoughts silently. Some might feel comfortable sharing personal details; others may be shy or even overwhelmed. You might need to remind the participants of this too, especially if someone is withholding for fear of judgment or criticism or another takes over because of a need to release their anxiety or painful emotion.

- For the participant who tends to dominate the discussion, it is important to step in. Be sure to cover that this might be necessary when you go over the ground rules in Session One, and ask the group for permission to step in. In the moment, speak directly to the participant by name, saying something like, *Jen, there is a lot to say about this and I wish we had time to hear it all. But could you bottom line it for us so that we can understand your point?* or *Keisha, we really appreciate that you are so willing to be open and to share. But it seems that you've gotten off track a bit. The question was…*

- A participant, acting out of fear or a sense of overwhelm, may hold back. She may be afraid of looking bad, especially if she has had multiple abortions, or that she won't give the 'right' answer. Encourage a reluctant talker by addressing her by name and asking her to refer to specific Reflection Exercises to express her thoughts. For example, *Nisha, what did you take away from the chapter on Loneliness? What could you relate to the most?* Active participation in the group is important, but always permit someone to pass if they choose not to share or to answer a particular question.

- A participant may be in the midst of a particularly painful or complicated personal situation and feel the need to talk about it in detail. This can overwhelm or distract the other participants and get the discussion off course. When it is clear that no resolution is forthcoming, jump in and suggest, *This is obviously a difficult situation, Lashawna. Let's all pray about this right now.* Then immediately lead the group in prayer.

NOTES

NOTES

PARTICIPANT INFORMATION FORM

Part 1: Background Information

Name: _____ Date: _____

Address: _____

City/State/Zip: _____

Phone: _____

Email: _____

Occupation: _____

Okay to call and leave voice mail? Yes _____ No _____

Okay to send you e-mail? Yes _____ No _____

Referred by/how did you hear about this group? _____
_____

Marital Status: Married _____ Single _____ Divorced _____ Widowed _____

Number and ages of children: _____
_____

When and how many abortions did you have? _____
_____
_____

Describe any help you have received to deal with your abortions: _____
_____
_____

What is most troubling to you right now about your abortion(s)? _____
_____
_____

What concerns you the most about participating in this support group? _____
_____
_____

How would you describe your spirituality? Are you a member of or attend a church? _____
_____

Book fee $_____ Will pay _____ Needs scholarship _____

Additional Notes: _____
_____

Part 2: Overview of the Group

Use the talking points below to explain the support group and to familiarize each participant with how it will work prior to attending the first session of the support group.

Describe the group.

- This is a support group for women who have experience with abortion. We will create a safe and supportive atmosphere so that you can explore how this experience has impacted, and may still be impacting your life.

- Even though it can be difficult to remember and talk about these experiences, avoiding pain does not bring healing. This group is a safe place where you will find tremendous compassion and support as you understand and grieve your loss.

- We study the book *Where Do Broken Hearts Go?* The author, Jane Abbate, experienced three abortions and knows personally the fear, guilt and pain you might be feeling. She shares her healing journey and how she has moved beyond her past to lead a good life.

- This study is grounded in a Christian perspective and offers helpful Bible references and prayer. However, you don't have to be 'religious' to benefit from this group or currently attend a church. We do ask that you be open to the possibility of developing or deepening a relationship with Jesus Christ.

- There are ___ weekly sessions. There is time in each session to share as little or as much of your experience as you choose. Perhaps unlike other small groups you may have attended in the past, understand that, in respect for all participants, attendance is mandatory. Note: This is a good time to review the dates of all sessions and/or to provide a copy of the meeting schedule.

- Confidentiality is required and you must commit protect the privacy of all participants.

Discuss that there is reading and preparation required for each session.

- Reading *WDBHG* is required. The *WDBHG Study Journal* is an optional resource. Advise that both books are available on amazon.com and inform if copies will be available for purchase at the first session. Provide scholarship information, if available.

- To help you get the most out of these sessions, each week you will be asked to read several book chapters and to complete the several exercises.
- In Session One, you will be asked to begin to tell your abortion story. It has been said that 'what can't be spoken can't be healed', so we hope you will trust us with your experience, knowing that everything you say will be held in strict confidence.

Encourage and acknowledge her courage.

- Reassure that God will honor her efforts and group leaders will support her every step.

Ask: Do you have any questions? Will you commit to attend all sessions?

NOTES

NOTES

MATERIALS LIST

The following is a list of supplies that will be needed in each of the group sessions.

Session One: My Heartbreak

- Handout: Accountability Covenant
- Handout: Meeting Schedule
- Handout: Sharing My Abortion Story
- Index cards or paper

Session Two: My Emotions

- Handout: The Feeling Wheel
- Pair of dice

Session Three: My Patterns and Triggers

None

Session Four: My Choices

- See-through cup/glass, ¾ full with water
- Box of food coloring
- Small flashlight
- Handout: Jesus: The Light of Life
- Pens and/or pencils
- Handout: Repeating Patterns

Session Five: My Relationships

- Small stones or rocks of varying shapes, sizes, colors, textures
- Pieces of rope cut in various lengths

Session Six: My Future

- Paper heart which can be torn into pieces
- Hearts of various shapes and sizes

NOTES

NOTES

MUSIC SUGGESTIONS

O
ne of the ways the Holy Spirit touches hearts is through the written and spoken Word of God. Another way can be through music that delivers God's promises of forgiveness, healing, and hope. Group leaders may choose to play music before, during, or after a session. If you choose to do so, be sure to provide copies of the song lyrics, which you can locate using Google.com. The following songs have been used in previous *WDBHG* support groups; feel free to choose any suitable music. Rely on the Spirit's inspiration and your best judgment if, and when, to use music to support the group's healing.

Session	Song Title	Artist
Session 1	If We Ever Needed You You're Not Alone I Need You to Love Me What Faith Can Do	Casting Crowns Meredith Andrews Barlow Girls Kutless
Session 2	Sweetly Broken At the Cross You Are Your Great Love	Jeremy Riddle Hillsong Colton Dixon Allison Park Worship
Session 3	Grace Flows Down Amazing Grace East to West When Mercy Found Me	Christy Nockels Chris Tomlin Casting Crowns Rhett Walker Bank
Session 4	Heal the Wound Healing Begins Never Once Not Guilty Anymore	Point of Grace Tenth Avenue North Matt Redman Aaron Keyes
Session 5	Free You Never Let Go Voice of Truth Mercy Said No	Steven Curtis Chapman Matt Redman Casting Crowns CeCe Winans
Session 6	All This Time I Can Only Imagine 10,000 Reasons Moving Forward Who Am I	Britt Nicole MercyMe Matt Redman Israel & New Breed Casting Crowns
These songs can be downloaded from iTunes for a small fee		

NOTES

NOTES

SAMPLE SCHEDULE

Where Do Broken Hearts Go?
Support Group

Note: All meetings are scheduled for 90 minutes

April 5   **My Heartbreak**
Introduction

April 12   **My Emotions**
Chapters 1, 2, 3, 8: Numbness, Heartbreak, Confusion,
Relief

April 19   **My Patterns and Triggers**
Chapters 4, 9, 10: Fear, Anger, Anxiety

April 26   **My Choices**
Chapters 5, 6, 12: Guilt, Shame, Regret

May 3   **My Relationships**
Chapters 7, 11, 13, 16: Loneliness, Envy, Courage, Freedom

May 10   **My Future**
Chapters 13-19: Courage, Love, Peace, Freedom, Gratitude,
Hope, Joy

Group Leader Contact Information:

Mary Smith
Mary@yahoo.com
444-222-8877

Sally Jones
Sally@yahoo.com
444-333-9922

Meeting Location:
Evangel Assembly
4532 Park Road
Columbia, PA 18823

NOTES

NOTES

SAMPLE FLYER

YOU CAN'T CHANGE YOUR PAST.
YOU CAN CHANGE YOUR FUTURE!

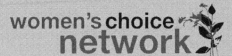

women's choice network

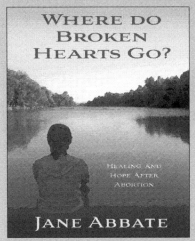

WHERE DO BROKEN HEARTS GO?

HEALING AND HOPE AFTER ABORTION

JANE ABBATE

POST ABORTION GROUP

START DATE: Every Tuesday
February 5 - March 12, 2014

TIME: 7:00 pm - 8:30 pm

LOCATION: Women's Choice Network
                    12705 Perry Highway Suite C
                    Wexford, PA 15090

GROUP LEADER: Jane Abbate, author of *Where Do Broken Hearts Go?*

TO REGISTER:

EMAIL: jane@messymiracles.com

or CALL: 412-953-9806

**If you reach voice mail leave your first name and a number that is ok to call you back. **

COST: Books will be provided. Suggested donation of $12 or go to www.amazon.com to purchase a Kindle edition

Confidential and Welcoming
Office is closed during your group

In a confidential, compassionate, small group setting we will cover topics such as how to:

- Break free from denial and confusion about your abortion experience
- Find relief from toxic guilt and shame
- Release and replace anger and anxiety with peace and hope
- Find comfort from feelings of heartbreak, regret, and loneliness
- Connect profoundly to the ultimate source of comfort and joy.

We understand it takes courage to reach out.

We hope you will trust that joining other women who share the abortion experience will make a positive difference in your life today and in your future.

NOTES

NOTES

ACCOUNTABILITY COVENANT

1. I am making this commitment to fully participate to the best of my ability in the *Where Do Broken Hearts Go?* support group.

2. I agree to *keep in confidence the names of all participants and group leaders*. I will respect everyone's privacy and *will not discuss any information from this group* with any individual outside of this group.

3. I agree to respect and value all participants of the group.

4. I will not interrupt, monopolize, or give advice.

5. I agree to attend all sessions. I will be on time and stay for the duration of the session. I have the freedom to end my participation in the group and if I do, I will contact the group leader and explain why. I agree not to just "disappear" without making some final contact.

6. I agree to call the group leader if I am unable to come to a meeting because of an emergency.

7. I agree to do the homework and participate fully in the group sessions.

Participant:

Name: _____

Date: _____

Signature: _____

Leader(s):

Name: _____

Date: _____

Signature: _____

NOTES

NOTES

NOTES

NOTES

Part 2

Group Leader
Outlines

SESSION ONE

MY HEARTBREAK

OVERVIEW

The goal is to establish relationships among women who have experienced abortion. Bonds of trust and compassion will slowly build as participants share their story and consider how abortion may have affected their lives. It is also important in this session to establish clear ground rules and expectations to protect confidentiality and encourage openness.

WELCOME AND INTRODUCTIONS

Opening Prayer:

The leader offers an opening prayer. Example: *Father God, we gather together as your daughters who have experienced the heartbreak of abortion. We are beginning a healing journey despite being afraid and full of shame. But we know that You love us and will be with us every step of the way. We thank You for Your Son, Jesus Christ, who paid the price for all that we have done. We pray that in the weeks ahead we will come to know Him more. Finally, we ask Your Holy Spirit to fill us with courage and strength so that we will seek and accept Your mercy and grace. Amen.*

Introductions:

Leader(s) begin the introductions by providing some of your personal background. Give a short explanation of your connection with abortion or the ways you have aborted God's will for your life. Explain why you chose to lead this study and your goals and hopes for the group. For example: *When I was 16 I had an abortion. It was very difficult to overcome my shame and guilt. Through support groups and counseling, I have been blessed to find healing and to be able to lead a good life. I know that is possible for you too and my goal is to support your healing in any way I can.*

Invite participants to provide a brief self-introduction. Remind them that they will be giving more details later in the session about their abortion experience. In this introduction ask each woman to tell what she would like the group to know about:

- Her name (participants do not have to reveal their full name)
- Her family
- Her occupation
- As you begin this support group, what are your expectations or hopes?

What to Expect:

Leader(s) explain the purpose of the group study: to explore and heal from the emotional impact of abortion and to draw closer to God.

- Distribute and review the schedule and dates of all the sessions.
- Distribute and review the *Accountability Covenant*.
- Describe how the material will be covered; for example, reading assignments, sharing and discussion, exercises, prayer, and/or music.
- Invite participants to ask questions or voice concerns.

Sharing Abortion Stories:

The process of sharing the story of your abortion experience with one another will help you to identify issues and events from your past that made you vulnerable to abortion or other regrettable choices. It can also surface areas of your life that need Christ's healing, transformative touch. Another benefit is that as you recognize similar patterns in your own life, compassion for yourself and others can grow.

It is important to keep in mind that, for many participants, it may be the first time they have spoken about their abortions. Ask the Holy Spirit to guide each participant in what she needs to remember and to talk about. Ask the group to receive each story with the utmost caring and respect. Remind participants that everything shared in the group is private and is to be kept confidential. Provide a few pointers on how to best listen to one another:

- Give one another your undivided attention.
- Do not interrupt.

- Avoid cross talk or commenting.
- Allow for a moment of silence after each participant concludes her story as a sign of respect.

While there is a great deal that each woman might share about her abortion experience, it is best to ask members to limit their sharing to 10-15 minutes each. Using the handout *Sharing My Abortion Story*, briefly review the points below. Invite the participants to choose the points that seem most important to discuss in the group. Allow time for the members to review the handout and prepare what they want to say.

Points to Cover:

- Describe your family, family life, your childhood, and the relationships among family participants.
- Was there divorce, alcoholism, or any form of abuse? (sexual, emotional, physical)
- How old were you when you experienced an unplanned pregnancy? Who knew about this situation?
- How did you make the decision to have an abortion? What circumstances or factors seemed most important at the time? Who, if anyone, was an influence in the decision?
- How did you get to the clinic or hospital? Was anyone with you? What do you remember about the procedure? What are your memories of how you got home and what you did afterward? What were your thoughts and feelings afterward?
- About 50% of women who have an abortion have more than one. If this is true for you, please share about all these losses.
- Who knows about the abortion(s)? What kind of support have you had from family, partners, and friends?
- What path has your life taken since the abortion(s)? How has abortion affected your life?

Leader Debrief Questions:

After all of the participants have finished telling their stories, allow time for group reflection. Do not permit participants to question one another about, *Why did you..?* or *Why didn't you?* Take your time and lead discussion through one or more of the following questions:

- What was it like to share your story? Did anything surprise you? Did you have any new insights? What did you notice as you listened to other women share their stories?

- What do you notice about how abortion has impacted you? Your relationships? Your physical, emotional, and mental health? Has there been an impact that's not included in that list?

- Why do you think now is the time to explore healing from your abortion?

Invite group members to review the questions on pages 10-13 in *WDBHG*. Inquire about the areas that seem to have had the greatest impact since the time of the abortion.

Healing Goal:

In the Bible we read about the prophet Elijah, who was sent to confront a king who rejected God. Elijah, like us, struggled with his feelings of fear and loneliness. He even tried to hide in a cave! In 1 Kings 19:9, God asked Elijah, *"What are you doing here?"* In this final part of today's session, you are asked to answer that question, *What are you doing here? What do you want God to do for you?*

- Distribute an index card and a pen/pencil to each participant. Ask participants to consider one area related to her abortion in which she would like to be healed and to write it on the index card. For example: *I have a lot of anger because of my abortions, especially towards myself. I want to learn how to forgive myself so that I can have a better life.* Another example: *My abortion has hardened my heart, causing me to be critical of others, especially my husband and children. I want to feel more loving towards my family and to believe I am worthy to be loved.*

- Allow a few minutes of quiet time for participants choose and write down their goal.

- Invite participants to share their healing goal with the group.

Ask participants to keep the index card in a safe place, perhaps inside their copy *WDBHG* or in a notebook. Remind participants that they will review this intention throughout the study.

Homework, Reflection, and Prayer:

Homework:

Read the Introduction and Chapters 1, 2, 3, and 8: Numbness, Heartbreak, Confusion and Relief in *WDBHG*. Complete the Reflection Exercises at the end of each chapter.

Reflection:

Invite each participant to briefly respond to one or more of the following questions, time allowing:

- What's the most significant thing that stood out to you tonight? It might be a new insight, feeling relief at telling your story, feeling encouraged/supported by others, etc.
- Do you have any further questions or concerns?
- Are you committed to continuing the study? Can we count on you?
- What else do you need to say?

Prayer:

Group leader may choose to lead this prayer or invite participants to lead and/or add to the final prayer.

Note:

Following the final prayer, distribute copies of *WDBHG* and the optional *WDBHG Study Journal* for purchase.

NOTES

NOTES

NOTES

NOTES

SHARING MY ABORTION STORY

The process of sharing the story of your abortion experience will help you identify issues and events from your past that made you vulnerable to abortion or other regrettable choices, and it will surface areas of your life that need the healing, transformative touch of Jesus Christ. Witnessing the stories of others can also build your own capacity for compassion. As you might recognize similar patterns and experiences of others in the group to your own, compassion can grow—for yourself and others.

This may be the first time you have spoken about your abortion. Ask the Holy Spirit to guide you in what you need to say, and be assured that the group leaders and members will receive your story with the utmost caring and respect.

Of course, anything shared in the group is to be kept confidential. Since we ask you to **limit your sharing to 10-15 minutes,** choose the points to cover (see below) that seem most important to discuss in the group.

Points to Cover:

- Describe your family, family life, your childhood, and the relationships among family participants.
- Was there divorce, alcoholism, or any form of abuse? (sexual, emotional, physical)
- How old were you when you experienced an unplanned pregnancy? Who knew about this situation?
- How did you make the decision to have an abortion? What circumstances or factors seemed most important at the time? Who, if anyone, was an influence in the decision?
- How did you get to the clinic or hospital? Was anyone with you? What do you remember about procedure? What are your memories of how you got home and what you did afterward? What were your thoughts and feelings afterward?

- About 50% of women who have an abortion have more than one. If this is true for you, please share about all these losses.
- Who knows about the abortion(s)? What kind of support have you had from family, partners, and friends?
- What path has your life taken since the abortion(s)? How has abortion affected your life?
- What else do you want to say?

NOTES

NOTES

NOTES

NOTES

SESSION TWO

MY EMOTIONS

OVERVIEW

Chapters 1, 2, 3, 8: Numbness, Heartbreak, Confusion, Relief

The goal is for participants to gain a better understanding of how emotions can impact behavior. There will be discussion about a wide range of emotions, and participants will be invited to identify the feelings that are most present for them as they reflect on their abortion experience. They will be encouraged to consider how acting on those emotions reaped an unfavorable impact on their life and those closest to them.

Getting Started:

Group leader welcomes the participants. Leader(s) explains that the purpose of this session is: to discover how abortion has impacted our lives—particularly our emotions—not just leading up to and immediately after the abortion but for the rest of our lives.

Opening Prayer:

Either the group leader or a participant offers a brief opening prayer. Example: *Father God, we invite You into our time together. We come before You with sincere hearts seeking to understand how abortion has impacted our lives. Please help us keep an open mind to what You would have us learn tonight about our emotions and how they have kept us apart from You. We pray for courage to face whatever comes up. We trust that You love us and are with us now and always. In the name of our Savior, Your Son, Jesus Christ. Amen.*

Opening Question:

How has our first meeting and telling your abortion story impacted you this week?

The Feeling Wheel—Exploring the Full Range of Your Emotions

As human beings, we have the potential to experience a full spectrum of emotions, both positive and negative ones. It may be surprising to notice the wide range of emotions that we are capable of feeling. (*For you created my inmost being; you knit me together in my mother's womb. I praise you because I am fearfully and wonderfully made; your works are wonderful, I know that full well.* Psalm 139:14-15, NIV)

The Feeling Wheel, developed by Dr. Gloria Willcox, identifies six primary feeling families: Sad, Mad, Scared, Joyful, Powerful, and Peaceful. Each feeling family has a spectrum of feelings within it. When something happens or you recall a memory, a feeling arises. You can use the Feeling Wheel to explore the layers of underlying emotions that are stirred up and more closely pinpoint what's going on for you.

For example, anger is a feeling related to mad and it can be accompanied by a sense of powerlessness. Relating this to your abortion could help you notice the anger you kept bottled up inside toward those involved with your abortion. Perhaps your anger sends you the message that you have been violated or taken advantage of in some ways. That may have led you to feel powerless to stand up for yourself when others insisted you have an abortion against your will.

You can also use the Feeling Wheel to expand your awareness of the wide range of emotions that are possible by exploring opposite feelings. Notice how the positive (Joyful, Powerful, Peaceful) feelings are opposite the negative (Sad, Mad, Scared) feelings. Now, notice that "Mad" and "Powerful" are opposing emotions from each side of the wheel.

As you reflect on this, you might ask yourself, *What do I need to feel more powerful in this relationship now?* That might lead you to explore setting or reestablishing some boundaries with these individuals. If you follow through on that, you might then begin to feel more positive emotions such as respected and valuable.

Emotional Healing from Abortion:

The group leader promotes discussion by asking an opening question such as: *Thinking over the past week, name one emotion that seemed to come up the most for you as you thought about your abortion experience.* Go around the circle and invite each woman to respond. Lead discussion that covers the points that follow.

- Abortion is more than a physical procedure; it is an emotional experience. There is not a right or wrong way to feel. Everyone is on their own unique healing journey and God has a plan for how this is to unfold. For some, discussing their abortions may cause a lot of tears, for others a lot of anger or anxiety. Whatever your experience, know that God will never give you anything more than you can handle (*The temptations in your life are no different from what others experience. And God is faithful. He will not allow the temptation to be more than you can stand. When you are tempted, he will show you a way out so that you can endure.* 1 Cor 10:13, NIV)

- Abortion affects us on many levels: physical, emotional, and spiritual. In this study, we're looking primarily at the wide variety of emotions that a woman might experience related to her abortion. While we will be focusing primarily on the ones from *WDBHG*, they are not the only ones that may come up for you. Just as the circumstances that led up to our abortion will vary, so might our emotional experience be different. What's most important is to understand how abortion affects our emotions so that we are not controlled by them. Instead, we can make conscious and intentional choices about how to respond to the variety of circumstances and people we face, regardless of how we feel about them in the moment.

  For example: When my best friend complains about her children, I might become angry because I resent the fact that she has children and I lost my only child through abortion. Rather than make a rude or sarcastic remark, I might simply acknowledge her frustration and then change the subject.

- Emotions are a gift from God. It is not sinful or inappropriate to express them. They are sources of information about what we are thinking and what drives our behavior. But emotions are also fleeting, sometimes changing by the moment. If we live by our emotions, we will be at the mercy of circumstances and other people. It's like rolling a pair of dice—you never know what you're going to face the day with. (Note: Leader may choose to roll dice several times as a way to illustrate the changing nature of our emotions.)

Exploring My Own Emotions:

Participants are invited to explore the emotions of: Numbness, Heartbreak, Confusion, and Relief. (Chapters 1, 2, 3, and 8 in *WDBHG*) Refer participants to their responses to the Reflection Exercises in each chapter and lead discussion through the following questions:

- *Numbness:*

  Referring to Chapter 1, what are you numbing; e.g. pain, guilt, shame? In what ways have you avoided or numbed your pain; e.g. overwork, drugs, alcohol, sex, shopping? Instead of numbing yourself to your pain, what might happen if you intentionally remembered the past? How would remembering be helpful? How might it make your life more difficult?

- *Heartbreak:*

  Referring to Chapter 2, what are the areas of your heartbreak; e.g. loneliness, never having children, negative self-image, etc.?

- *Confusion:*

  Referring to Chapter 3, what remains unclear or confusing to you about your abortion experience; e.g. not remembering the dates/details, why I didn't think I could handle having a baby, etc.?

- *Relief:*

  Referring to Chapter 8, how did abortion solve a problem or a burden? What did abortion help you to avoid; e.g. admitting to an affair or having premarital sex, etc.?

- Why do we sometimes try to avoid or hide our hurt and pain? Why is it difficult to be real with other people? In what ways have you tried to hide your feelings from God?

- What else stood out in your homework reading? Which of these emotions seems more dominant for you then, and now? Refer to The Feeling Wheel. What other emotions are running your life?

A New Way to Live: By Faith, Not By Emotion:

Though Holy Scripture encourages us to be real and honest about our emotions, they never tell us to live by them. The truth of God's Word is our authority, *not* our feelings. This doesn't mean that we should deny, repress, or hide our feelings. We should express them to God and pray for guidance as to how He would have us respond.

Some might wonder how to strengthen their faith and reduce dependence on feelings. Ask participants what helps them to do so. Invite the participants to consider the alternatives to living based on your emotions:

- Regular Bible reading. There are many options to study the Bible in printed form, online and through smartphone apps. Suggestions include the You Version (bible.com) and Bible Gateway (biblegateway.com) *(There's nothing like the written Word of God for showing you the way to salvation through faith in Christ Jesus. Every part of Scripture is God-breathed and useful one way or another—showing us truth, exposing our rebellion, correcting our mistakes, training us to live God's way. Through the Word we are put together and shaped up for the tasks God has for us. 2 Timothy 3: 16—17, MSG)*

- Daily Prayer. There's really no right or wrong way to pray. Don't worry about fancy words or making it sound good. Just tell Jesus what's on your mind and heart and be assured that He is listening to you. If you feel stuck, you can pray the way Jesus taught us in Matthew 6:9-13, NIV:

Our Father in heaven, hallowed be Your name, Your kingdom come, Your will be done, on earth as it is in heaven. Give us today our daily bread. And forgive us our debts, as we also have forgiven our debtors. And lead us not into temptation, but deliver us from the evil one.

- Journaling. This is the perfect time to begin recording the thoughts, emotions, actions, questions, learning, etc. that begin to arise as you reflect deeply on your abortion experience. The Holy Spirit has a way of speaking to you as you pour out words on the page. Keep your journal with you or download one of the free smartphone apps to make note of memories and thoughts as they come to mind.

- Support groups. Some participants may be dealing with a variety of ongoing difficulties beyond abortion including abuse, addiction, financial, etc. Support groups bring together people facing similar issues, and, like this small group, participants may benefit from joining another group. Group leaders may choose to have the contact information for a variety of support networks such as AA, OA, NA, ASCA.

- Counseling. The *WDBHG* support group is not a substitute for professional therapy. Participants may find counseling with a professional, licensed therapist an essential part of the recovery and healing process. Group leaders may choose to have the contact information for several local therapists available for referral.

Homework, Reflection, and Prayer:

Homework:

Read Chapters 4, 9, and 10: Fear, Anger, and Anxiety in *WDBHG*. Complete the Reflection Exercises at the end of each chapter.

Reflection:

Invite each participant to briefly respond to the following:

- What's the most significant thing that stood out to you tonight?
- What else do you need to say?

Prayer:

Group leader may choose to lead this prayer but may invite members to lead and/or add to final prayer. Be sure to ask God for His blessing over the healing goals that the participants have identified.

The Feeling Wheel

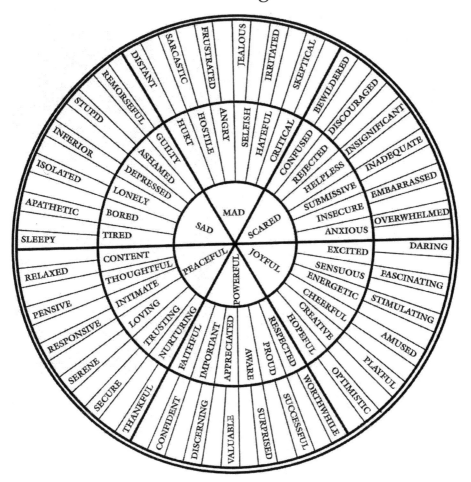

The Feeling Wheel was developed by Dr. Gloria Willcox. In a given situation, use the Feeling Wheel to identify the root of your emotions in one of the six "core" feelings: Sad, Mad, Scared, Joyful, Powerful, and Peaceful. Then you can explore the layers of underlying feelings to more closely pinpoint what's going on for you.

As you are about to begin this journey and explore your abortion experience, you might be filled with many emotions. Using the Feeling Wheel above, circle the emotions you are most aware of right now. What emotions were most present during and around the time of your abortion? What are the impacts of these feelings on your well-being, your relationships with others, your relationship with Jesus?

NOTES

NOTES

NOTES

NOTES

Session Three
My Patterns and Triggers

OVERVIEW

Chapters 4, 9, 10: Fear, Anger, Anxiety

In previous sessions, participants began to explore the wide variety of emotions that may follow an abortion. In this session, the focus is on three very common emotions: fear, anger, and anxiety. The group will discuss what triggers these emotions and learn a coping method to increase self-awareness and self-control.

Opening Prayer:

Either the group leader or a participant offers a brief opening prayer. Example: *Lord Jesus, we continue to dig deeper into the difficult feelings we have experienced as a result of our abortions. It is not an easy thing to do and we need Your help to remain calm, patient, and focused. Because of Your grace, we can surrender to the power and embrace the presence of the Holy Spirit. Father God, I have been down a difficult path, making lots of mistakes and hurting myself and others in the process. But rather than continue down that path, I am stopping right now and asking You to change me. Help me to become the woman you plan for me to be. We ask this in the name of Your Son, and our Savior, Jesus Christ. Amen.*

Opening Question:

Which emotion do you associate most with your abortion experience: anger or fear?

Exploring Difficult Emotions:

Just because we feel fear, anger or anxiety, that does not mean there is always a connection to abortion. However, in this study we want to explore the times when these difficult emotions are, in fact, triggered by events and relationships related to our abortion experience. Lead discussion about the participants' sense of fear, anger and anxiety by asking the following questions:

Fear: (Refer to WDBHG *Reflection Exercise p. 34–35)*

- Recall the people and/or circumstances that caused you to be afraid in the time leading up to, during, and after your abortion experience. What did your fears have in common? In what ways do you currently experience fear related to your abortion, for example: fear that certain people will find out, fear of infertility or miscarriage. How do you typically react when you are afraid? What results do these fears produce in your life?

Anger: (Refer to WDBHG *Reflection Exercise p. 70–72)*

- Research shows that when you are angry you lose access to up to 80% of your effective intelligence. Can you recall a time when you erupted in anger and said hurtful things? Why do you think you flew off the handle with that individual? What unresolved anger do you still hold toward those involved in your abortion or the people that represent them to you? How has anger over your abortion affected you (e.g., relationships, career, physically, safety-wise, financially, etc.)?

Anxiety: (Refer to WDBHG *Reflection Exercise p. 79-81)*

- There is a difference between worry and anxiety. We experience worry in relation to a specific event, but anxiety is a sense of foreboding or uneasiness, not necessarily associated with something in particular. Anxiety is a general feeling of being upset. Have you ever experienced chronic anxiety, panic attacks, phobias and fears, obsessive-compulsive behaviors? How might they be associated with your abortion experience?

Triggers: What Is Driving You?

You have good intentions to be faithful, to exercise self-control, and to trust God. But things (and people) can get in your way and 'trigger' an unwanted or overwhelming emotion. Triggers create an emotional reaction that can hijack you from behaving or responding in the way you intend.

For example, if I'm riding in a car with my husband and spot a sign that reads, 'Abortion is Murder,' I get tense and criticize him for driving too fast. We end up in an argument because I am not aware that those kinds of signs trigger guilt and self-loathing. My husband has now become a victim of my misplaced anxiety and emotion.

The group leader can expand the awareness of what triggers difficult feelings related to abortion and how they can hijack behavior by leading discussion with the following questions:

- What triggers difficult feelings in you related to your abortion? (Refer to the Reflection Exercise on p. 10–13 for possible ideas.)
- How can you tell you are being hijacked? What are the physical signs? What does your body language show? How are your thoughts impacted? How do you typically feel?
- What normally happens when you become hijacked? What familiar patterns of behavior do you find yourself falling into? How do you get yourself under control? If not, what happens? What's the impact?
- How can being aware of your triggers help you?

Despite our best intentions to respond in the right way while under stress, remember that the enemy, Satan, will do everything in his power to keep us from trusting God and believing in His mercy and love. Satan wants to control your thoughts and your emotions, everything you say and do, to interfere with your relationship with God. Particularly as you seek healing from your abortion wounds, Satan will want to keep you down. He does this by making you fearful, which often causes anger and anxiety. (*The thief's purpose is to steal and kill and destroy. My purpose is to give them a rich and satisfying life.* John 10:10, NLT)

The Pause:

There are many ways that negative, destructive thought patterns can control our lives and steal our peace. In the process of healing from abortion, it is not unusual for something or someone to trigger a memory and restart your emotional roller coaster. By understanding what those triggers are and being prepared before you react, you can calm yourself, allowing you to put on the brakes, shift gears, and regroup. Without it, you might rush ahead and react before you've had a chance to fully think through what you want to do or say. Or, you may get stuck in a self-destructive pattern of thinking.

To help participants avoid these self-defeating reactions, the group leader can teach an effective technique—The Pause. After explaining the following five-step process, ask participants to recall a recent difficult situation at work or home. Slowly lead the participants through each step, inviting them to practice The Pause. Discuss the outcome and impact.

1. *Practice physical awareness in the moment.* Identify sensations like tension, a pounding heart, tears springing to your eyes, light-headedness, or fury. Notice where they occur in your body and give them a name: *I am shaking and feeling sick to my stomach.*

2. *Practice emotional awareness.* Attach an emotion to the sensations you are feeling. For example, say to yourself, *I am furious* or *I am overwhelmed.* Naming your feeling will help prevent you from being overwhelmed by your emotions and feeling out of control.

3. *Breathe.* Close your mouth. Count to eight while breathing slowly and deeply through your nose. Gently let the air out through your mouth. Focusing on your breathing helps to calm and slow you down. Repeat this over and over.

4. *Redirect your attention.* Make some physical movement immediately as you breathe. For example, remove your glasses, take a sip of coffee or water, cross or uncross your legs.

5. *Repeat a calming phrase.* Silently, to yourself, repeat a few words or phrase that you have pre-selected while breathing and performing the physical movement. Examples: *I am okay* or *I can handle this.* Calling to mind a short prayer such as *Help me Jesus* or a Bible verse such as Psalm 56:3, *When I am afraid, I will put my trust in you,* will help to calm and compose you.

Homework, Reflection, and Prayer:

Homework:

Read Chapters 5, 6, and 12: Guilt, Shame, and Regret in *WDBHG*. Complete the Reflection Exercises at the end of each chapter.

Refer to the Reflection Exercise on p.10–13 in *WDBHG* to gain a better understanding of your triggers. Consider what people and/or circumstances are more likely to set off a negative emotional reaction. Create a calming phrase. Look for an opportunity to practice The Pause this week.

Reflection:

- Review the healing intention you wrote on an index card during Session One. What progress are you making in this area? How is God working in your life to help you with this?
- What else do you need to say?

Prayer:

Group leader may choose to lead this prayer but may invite members to lead and/or add to final prayer. Be sure to ask God for His blessing over the healing goals that the participants have identified.

NOTES

NOTES

NOTES

NOTES

NOTES

SESSION FOUR
MY CHOICES

OVERVIEW

Chapters 5, 6, 12: Guilt, Shame, Regret

When we begin to deal with the sin of abortion and bring it into the light, it is perfectly natural to experience uncomfortable feelings of guilt, shame, and regret. These difficult emotions can be overwhelming and cause us to lose hope of ever being forgiven—by family and friends, our aborted child, God. We may find it most difficult to forgive ourselves.

In this session participants examine how falling into the sin of abortion has clouded their life, kept them down and prevented them from becoming all God has created them to be. The good news is that we have a choice: We can either fall into the darkness of condemnation or rise up to accept the light of God's mercy and grace.

Opening Prayer:

Either the group leader or a participant offers a brief opening prayer. Example: *Jesus, You said that You are the light of the world and that if we follow You, we won't have to stumble around in the darkness of sin and condemnation (John 8:12). We ask that You shine Your merciful and loving light into our hearts tonight. May it lead us to see the parts of us that have been darkened by the guilt and shame of abortion. We believe that You have the light that leads to life. Please light our path to You tonight. In Your name, Jesus, we pray. Amen.*

Opening Question:

For homework this week, you were asked to identify your triggers and to practice a calming phrase. What are your triggers? What is your calming phrase?

Exercise—The Light of Life

Set up:

Be sure to practice the following exercise ahead of time to become familiar with the activity and necessary props. If possible, it is desirable to have a sink and running water nearby, or, adapt the exercise to what's available for you.

The following supplies are needed for this exercise:

1. A see-through plastic cup/glass filled with water
2. A box of food coloring
3. A small flashlight
4. Pens and/or pencils
5. Handout: Jesus: The Light of Life handout

Gather the participants around a table with the glass of water, food coloring and flashlight visible to everyone. Distribute a pen or pencil and *Jesus: The Light of Life* handout. Explain that this activity is an interactive exercise designed to explore the influence of guilt and shame have had in our lives. Guide participants through this exercise, paraphrasing in your own words, the following explanation.

Begin Demonstration:

We would all like to see ourselves like this cup of bright, clear water. It's full of light and life. God's light can shine right through (use a flashlight and shine it through the side of the cup).

We were once that person before our innocence was gone. But there came a time in our lives when we compromised good values and chose abortion. And darkness entered in. (Add 6 to 8 drops of the food coloring.)

This "choice" may have been followed with lies and deceit to hide and cover up what we did, and the darkness in our souls increased. (Add more drops of food coloring.)

Just when we thought that we could put it all behind us and get back to some kind of normal life, something new entered... the darkness of post-abortion trauma. (Add more drops food coloring.) Guilt and shame entered our life. We became aware of many regrets and lost opportunities. (Add a few more drops of food coloring.)

And little did we know that this darkness also was leading to a new mindset. We began to believe that our sin was so wrong and we were so horrible that God could not and would not forgive us. That He no longer loved us. So we began to hide from Him and avoid His light. Maybe we stopped going to church, or stopped praying. Maybe we tried different religions and spiritual practices. Maybe we got caught up with addictions or sexual promiscuity. Maybe we didn't want our lives exposed to God's light because we were afraid of what would be revealed. (*All who do evil hate the light and refuse to go near it for fear their sins will be exposed. But those who do what is right come to the light so others can see that they are doing what God wants.* John 3:20–21, NLT)

But we learned that staying in the darkness only leads to more darkness. (Add more drops of food coloring.) And darkness is a huge bondage. Huge! (PAUSE)

We did the best we could, while the enemy kept throwing more barriers and obstructions at us; we felt condemned and hopeless. A life filled with guilt, shame, and self-condemnation is a very dark place. There is no light in the soul filled with condemnation. (Shine the flashlight against the side of the cup. The light will not be visible through to the other side.)

Without the Holy Spirit, we remain in darkness. (Hold up the darkened cup. PAUSE)

What are some of the ways we handle the darkness?

- We became perfectionists, people pleasers, super mom, super wife, super employee, and so on.
- We may have used drugs, promiscuity, addictions, cutting, and harmful behaviors to numb and help cope with the darkness.

These behaviors might have numbed us to the pain, helped us feel better about ourselves in some ways—but they did not take the guilt and shame away. There may have been some bright moments, even for days on end, but it was never very long before the darkness set in again.

Pause:

Ask the women to prayerfully consider their own darkness. Refer to *Jesus: The Light of Life* handout and invite them to make note of the areas of guilt, shame, and regret they have experienced.

Questions:

- What is the connection between darkness and your abortion experience?
- In what ways do you feel guilt about your abortion?
- How has shame impacted your life?
- What are your deepest regrets?
- What other areas of darkness are present in your life right now?

Resume Demonstration:

Over time, we began to realize that we can't create our own light—no matter who we are or what we do. We can't make it all better on our own. No person or relationship, no amount of good behavior, money, success, and intelligence can re-create the light we desperately want and need in our lives. But, we have been given a Savior who can!

(Invite the participants to follow you to a sink and begin to run water into the cup as you continue the activity. Allow water to run until the dark water is completely flushed out and replaced with clear water.)

When we confess our sins and accept Jesus as our Lord and Savior, He begins to flush out our darkness and we get filled with the light of Christ. (*The people who walk in darkness will see a great light. For those who live in a land of deep darkness, a light will shine.* Isaiah 9:2, NLT)

You may notice that it took time for the dark water to be totally clear. So it will be with our healing and recovery from abortion. It will take more than a six-week study or a healing retreat. As we follow Jesus and deepen our relationship with Him, more and more darkness fades. And now if we shine that flashlight behind the cup again, we can see that the light of Christ can once again shine through us! (Shine the flashlight through the side of the cup) This is the hope that is in Christ—the hope that draws us together right now.

In the moment we confess our abortion and accept Jesus as our Lord and Savior, He forgives our sin and the darkness of abortion is replaced with His light. Even better, God wants each of us to reflect His light into the world and that is why we know we have a future and a hope!

Questions:
- What is possible for you now as your darkness is replaced with the light of Christ?
- What do you need to be able to reflect God's light?

Conclusion:

Invite participants to reflect on the powerful healing that our Lord and Savior offers to each one of us. You may choose to have some music playing softly in the background while they consider this wonderful gift. Conclude with a summary such as the following:

The darkness of evil never has and never will extinguish God's light. Jesus Christ is God's light in this world. With His light, we are able to see the sinners we really are. He removes the darkness of sin from our lives. Then He lights the path ahead of us so we can see how to live! If you let Christ guide your life, you'll never need to stumble in the darkness of guilt, shame, and regret again! (*The Word gave life to everything that was created, and his life brought light to everyone. The light shines in the darkness, and the darkness can never extinguish it.* John 1:4–5, NLT)

Note: The group leader may sense that this exercise may inspire a participant to surrender her life to Christ. If that is the case, lead her in a prayer of salvation such as the following:

Father God, I know that my abortion was a sin and that it has driven a wedge between us. I am truly sorry and I deeply regret my abortion. I am leaving my past behind and turning my heart over to you. Please forgive me and help me not to sin again.

I believe that your Son, Jesus Christ, died for my sins, was resurrected from the dead, and is alive and hears my prayers. I invite Jesus to capture my heart and rule in my life from this day forward.

Homework Preparation:

In the next group session, participants will explore the impact of repeating patterns of behavior in their life and relationships. The leader informs the group that, in addition to the normal homework reading assignment, there is an exercise to be completed.

The leader asks, *"Did you ever hear the phrase, 'History repeats itself'"?* Human beings develop habits for daily routines such as, *I always sleep on the same side of the bed and take the same routes to work and to the mall.* We also develop patterns in our interaction with others such as, *I really want to be in a good relationship but I keep picking losers!*

Discuss how, whether we notice it or not, we create certain patterns in our lives. Sometimes, when we look more closely at our behavior, we notice these patterns are not producing the quality of life we want. Often, our behavior is producing the opposite of what we really desire. This is an example of a self-defeating or self-sabotaging pattern.

Review the *Repeating Patterns* handout, or the leader may substitute an example of a way she repeats behavior that results in the opposite of what she really wants. Invite the participants to prayerfully reflect during the next week on the choices and behaviors they tend to cycle through over and over in their life.

Homework, Reflection, and Prayer:

Homework:

Read Chapters 7, 11, 13, 16: Loneliness, Envy, Courage and Freedom in *WDBHG.* Complete the Reflection Exercises at the end of each chapter.

Complete the Repeating Patterns handout.

- Reflect upon the people who were involved in your abortion. Consider how your abortion impacted those relationships. What happened to those relationships? Who is most affected by your abortion history today?

Reflection:

Ask each participant to briefly respond to the following:

- What's the most significant thing that stood out to you tonight?
- What else do you need to say?

Prayer:

End with prayer. Group leader may choose to lead this prayer but may invite members to lead and/or add to the final prayer.

NOTES

NOTES

JESUS: THE LIGHT OF LIFE

In this exercise, the water glass below represents your life. Take a few minutes to consider what actions you took that have caused your guilt. What are you most ashamed of about yourself? What are your deepest regrets? How much guilt, shame, and regret have filled your life? Is your glass ¼, ½, ¾, or totally filled with these emotions?

We sometimes try to protect ourselves from feelings of guilt and shame by putting our faith in something we do or have such as our good deeds, skill or intelligence, money or possessions. But only God can save us from eternal condemnation. Where have you turned to in the past in an effort to 'make up' for your sins?

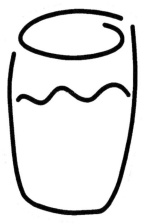

As Jesus flushes out the darkness, we are filled with more and more of his light. *(The people who walk in darkness will see a great light. For those who live in a land of deep darkness, a light will shine. Isaiah 9:2, NLT)*

What is possible for you now that the darkness is diminished and the light of Christ is shining through?

Pray:

Jesus, You are the light of the world. The darkness of evil never has and never will extinguish Your light. With Your light I am able to see the sinner I really am. Only You can remove the darkness of sin from my life and light the path ahead of me so that I can truly live! Jesus, I am so sorry for my sin. I invite You into my life to guide every step and decision. I never want to stumble in the darkness of guilt, shame, and regret again! *(The Word gave life to everything that was created, and his life brought light to everyone. The light shines in the darkness, and the darkness can never extinguish it. John 1:4–5, NLT)*

NOTES

NOTES

NOTES

NOTES

REPEATING PATTERNS

Reflect upon the patterns of your behavior throughout your life. Some patterns produce good results, such as working hard and earning promotions. At other times, notice how you keep doing something that produces disappointing or hurtful results, such as lending money to family members who never pay you back. Focus on *your* behavior and how it seems to end in loss, pain, grief, shame, guilt, fear, sadness, or a sense of defeat. The similarity in negative results from each cycle tells you this is a 'repeating pattern' and not just a run of bad luck. The following are some examples that point to a self-defeating pattern:

- Instead of learning by my mistakes, I repeat the same mistake, expecting a different result.

- I keep getting involved in the same kind of unsatisfactory relationship (family, business, or personal) again and again with the same kinds of unsuitable partners. Each time it turns out to benefit them but not me. Once I'm in it I can't seem to get myself out.

- I repeatedly suffer physical, mental, sexual, or other kinds of abuse.

- When in a bad situation, I fantasize about magical or super-powerful ways to get back to a better life, such as winning the lottery, finding a new lover who will fix everything, or plotting revenge by committing an unhealthy or illegal activity.

- My finances are a mess. I live beyond my means and keep getting into debt.

- I regularly find myself in a state of powerlessness, feeling that I can't do anything about it.

- I am unable to focus on a career. I change jobs frequently or I constantly feel either overwhelmed or underutilized at work.

REPEATING PATTERN EXAMPLE

The consequences of Sarah's behavior were two unplanned pregnancies and two abortions. Lack of awareness of our patterns and their impact can lead to repeated pain and suffering.

MY REPEATING PATTERNS

Draw an example of one of your own self-defeating patterns.

Reflection Questions:

- What are the significant features of my pattern?

- How does this pattern impact my life? Who else does it impact and why?

- How might this pattern relate to my abortion experience and what followed?

- Is this loop of self-defeating behavior still present in my life today? If so, what am I doing, perhaps unconsciously, that might continue to bring these same unpleasant experiences to me? If not, what has broken the cycle?

- What do I want Jesus to do for me to help stop this self-defeating cycle?

NOTES

NOTES

NOTES

NOTES

NOTES

SESSION FIVE
MY RELATIONSHIPS

OVERVIEW

Chapters 7, 11, 13, 16: Loneliness, Envy, Courage, Freedom

The effects of abortion are long lasting and impact many areas of a woman's life. The goal of this session is to explore how a woman's relationships may be impacted by abortion.

Opening Prayer:

Either the group leader or a participant offers a brief opening prayer. Example: *Father God, You created us to be in relationship with You, to love and glorify You. You created in us a desire for emotional, physical, and spiritual connection with other people. Tonight, we reflect on the important relationships in our lives that have been affected by abortion. We pray that You would help us to take responsibility for our words, actions, and attitudes so that we might understand their consequences and the effect they have on others. We also pray that You will reveal to us those relationships that do not honor You and give us the courage to let go and move on. Amen.*

Opening Question:

In your homework you were asked to identify any repeating patterns that relate to your abortion experience. What new insights did you gain about the impact these patterns have had and/or currently have on your life?

The Value of Relationships:

The group leader provokes discussion by asking the following question:

What do the following three things have in common?

1. *Buying a cup of coffee at Starbucks*

2. *Driving your car on a crowded freeway*

3. *Having a tooth pulled*

This isn't a trick question! Participants can have some fun guessing the answer. But the 'correct' answer is: *They all involve relationships!* Ask participants what qualities of relationships are important in the all of the above? e.g. trust, self-control, respect, patience, etc.

We need relationships to get basic needs met, like interacting with the clerk to place and pay for our order at the coffee shop. We also have to cooperate with one another while driving in heavy traffic (well, at least some of us do!) so that we all arrive safely at our destinations. And we certainly want a trusting relationship with our dentist when we are facing a painful procedure.

*The LORD God said, "It is not good for the man to be alone. I will make a helper suitable for him." (*Genesis 2:18, NLT*)* He wired us to need relationships. From the moment we are born, we are in relationship with our parents, siblings, and other relatives. Soon we are forming relationships with other children. As we go through life, we make connections with people at school and work, develop friendships, and eventually may marry and create new relationships with our own children. In fact, there's no escaping relationship!

Exercise: The Relationships Involved in Your Abortion(s):

Gather the participants around a table. In the center of the table, place an assortment of stones. (Note: Small bags of stones can be purchased at a craft supply store, typically in the floral department.) There should be enough stones for each woman to choose about three to six stones, although be sure to have extras on hand.

Begin with the following explanation:

Tonight we are going to reflect on the people who played a part in our abortion experience. Take a few minutes and consider all of those people who bear some responsibility. For example, you might choose: yourself, the father of the baby, God, a friend who encouraged you, the doctor, etc. What relationships were you trying to protect, save, or avoid by having an abortion?

Choose one stone to represent each person that comes to mind. You may have as few as one stone, or many stones, depending on your view of who shares the responsibility for your abortion. After everyone has made their selections, we invite you to comment briefly about whom the stones represent and how they share responsibility for what occurred.

As they are ready, the participants will choose stones and, after everyone has made their selections, ask:

- None of us experienced our abortion in isolation. Tell us about who you see as responsible for your situation and what their role was. Who would like to start?

After each participant has had a chance to speak, ask some or all of the following questions:

- Choose one or two people. How did their involvement in your abortion play out in your relationship? What ultimately happened to the relationship?
- What emotions were most often present in these relationships, e.g. anger, love, shame, disappointment, loneliness, etc.?
- How did your relationship with these individuals impact your interactions with other people? How do they affect your relationships now?

The Courage and Freedom to Choose Your Relationships:

Abortion can have a significant impact on your relationships—not just with the people involved at the time but also with people you met later in life who represented them to you. For example, if you felt abandoned by the father of your child and had to face abortion alone, you might be cautious around all men and regard them all as weak or uncaring. As a result, you might eventually find it difficult to bond with your husband and fully trust him.

At one extreme, post-abortive women may isolate themselves, fearful of disapproval and rejection. At the other extreme, promiscuity may be a way some post-abortive women attempt to re-create a more loving and attentive relationship with a man.

Referring back to the beginning of the session when we discussed that relationships are not optional, consider your *current* experience with relationships.

- Why is it a blessing that you cannot escape relationships?
- Spend some time thinking about your relationship with yourself. How much are you affected by your abortion and how you see yourself as a result? Is your overall self-image an asset or liability in your relationships with others? What changes do you need to make in the way you see yourself?

Connecting or Letting Go

The group leader will use a short piece of rope to illustrate the following; providing a piece of rope for each participant is optional.

In Ecclesiastes 4:9–12 (MSG), God said: *It's better to have a partner than go it alone. Share the work, share the wealth. And if one falls down, the other helps, but if there's no one to help, tough! Two in a bed warm each other. Alone, you shiver all night. By yourself you're unprotected. With a friend you can face the worst. Can you round up a third? A three-stranded rope isn't easily snapped.*

This Scripture reminds us that life is designed for companionship, not isolation; for intimacy, not loneliness. After being hurt, abandoned, or disappointed by people involved in her abortion experience, some women might prefer solitude, comfortable with its familiarity and safety. Since we were created not to serve ourselves but to serve God and others, invite group discussion using some of the following questions:

- Choose a relationship where you desire greater connection and intimacy. (Leader demonstrates by holding one end of a rope and offering the other end to a group member to hold on to.) Who is that person? If you could hope for this to be the very best relationship, what would be different? How can you connect with this person in a deeper, more genuine and fulfilling way?
- Choose a relationship that drains you, frustrates you, or causes you to frequently be in turmoil. What is your part in the difficulty? From Ecclesiastes 3:1–8 we learn that there's a right time for everything. Are you in a tug-of-war with someone and it's time to drop the rope? (Leader demonstrates by tugging on the rope and the other person pulls

back.) Is it time for this relationship to end? Or, is it time for you to take responsibility for your part of the difficulty and give up or stop a certain attitude, belief, or behavior toward the other person?

Homework, Reflection, and Prayer:

Homework:

- Read Chapters 13 through 19: Courage, Love, Peace, Freedom, Gratitude, Hope, Joy in *WDBHG*. Complete the Reflection Exercises at the end of each chapter.

Reflection:

Invite each participant to briefly respond to the following:

- What's the most significant thing that stood out to you tonight?
- What else do you need to say?

Prayer:

Group leader may choose to lead this prayer but may invite members to lead and/or add to the final prayer. Add a special prayer focus by asking God to heal the participants' difficult or broken relationships.

NOTES

NOTES

NOTES

SESSION SIX
MY FUTURE

OVERVIEW

Chapters 13, 14, 15, 16, 17, 18, 19: Courage, Love, Peace, Freedom, Gratitude, Hope, Joy

Participants have explored 19 emotions that are frequently associated with the experience of abortion. God has given us the gift of emotions as messengers of what we are thinking and what is driving our behavior. Reaching into the past, uncovering difficult and often repressed memories, reflecting on our heartbreaks and disappointments has not been easy. Yet, God promised that we will be rewarded for our faithfulness and efforts to heal. He wants to mend our broken hearts so that we can grow and become emotionally mature and healthy. As we allow God to change our hearts, we are preparing ourselves so that He may use us in a positive way—even our experience of abortion!

Opening Prayer:

Either the group leader or a participant offers a brief opening prayer. Example: *Dear Father, we come to You again, seeking healing for our emotional wounds. The experience of abortion has stirred up many difficult and painful emotions and smothered other feelings that could restore peace and hope. We ask You now to continue to transform us so that even this darkest part of our past could be used to glorify You. In the words of your servant Paul, spoken many years ago, we offer this prayer, confident "that he who began a good work in you will carry it on to completion until the day of Christ Jesus"* (Philippians 1:3–6). *Amen.*

Opening Question:

What are your greatest hopes and dreams for the future?

Exercise: A Change of Heart

The group leader uses a paper heart that has been cut from red craft paper to demonstrate how abortion and hurtful emotions damaged and broke our hearts. Invite the participants to reflect on the areas of heartbreak and hurtful emotions they experienced because of their abortions. Ask the group to respond to the following questions:

- During the past six weeks, which emotions do you most closely associate with your abortion experience? How have these emotions impacted your life? (Note: As emotions are named, e.g., heartbreak, guilt, shame, etc., the group leader tears off small pieces of the paper heart.)
- What happens when you operate out of a torn and damaged heart?
- What was the impact of your heartbreak on you? Your relationships?

Emphasize that it is normal to have difficult and painful feelings. The key is to acknowledge them, rather than deny or suppress them or to numb yourself through self-destructive behaviors.

The leader should shift the tone and announce with enthusiasm that there is good news! Although you may have hid your abortion from other people, and even justified it to yourself, Jesus knows the condition of your heart *now*. The prophet Ezekiel had predicted thousands of years ago that there would be a time when you would reach out in desperation and Jesus would give you a heart transplant!

The group leader presents a new heart to each participant, cut from red craft paper or something similar, with the following or comparable Scripture written on it: *I will take away their stony, stubborn heart and give them a tender, responsive heart. (*Ezekiel 11:19–20b, NLT) Emphasize how much Jesus loves them and wants to be in relationship with them. Invite participants to consider how, with this new heart, the future could be different.

- Now, as you look ahead, what is possible if you operate from this new, tender, responsive heart?
- What are your dreams for the future? What are God's plans for you?

- If you don't know, what can you do to 'seek Him with all your heart' (Jeremiah 29:13)?
- How do you think your wound of abortion enhances your usefulness to God?
- What unfinished business do you have now? What's your next step in healing your emotional wounds caused by abortion?
- What do you need to surrender to Christ to take care of so that you can continue to heal?
- What good can come from sharing your story with people you trust? How will you know if and when it is time to share? Who most needs to know? (Refer to WDBHG, p. 103)

Homework, Reflection, and Prayer

Reflection:

Ask each participant to briefly respond to the following:

- Refer to the healing intention you wrote during our first meeting. In what ways has God answered your prayers? How have you been blessed during this time? How has your relationship with God changed?
- What do you most want to remember about this healing journey? What can you do to make sure you do so?
- What do you need to say to be complete with this experience?

Prayer:

A very special and personal way to conclude this support group would be for the leader(s) to approach each participant and pray specifically over each individual. Invite all participants to pray with you. Recall some of the deepest wounds that were expressed. Pray for additional revelation and the resources and support that will be necessary for continued healing. Call each woman forth by declaring God's blessing over her life (refer to *WDBHG,* pp. 134–137).

NOTES

NOTES

NOTES

PART 3

RESOURCES

RESOURCES

Healing from abortion is a process and takes time—probably a lifetime. Participation in a support group is one important step. The following resources will support the ongoing journey of healing and hope.

Small Group and Self-Study Abortion Healing Resources:

Rachel's Vineyard
www.rachelsvineyard.org

Forgiven and Set Free
By: Linda Cochrane

Healing a Father's Heart
By: Linda Cochrane and Kathy Jones

SaveOne: A Guide to Emotional Healing After Abortion
SaveOne: The Men's Study
By: Sheila Harper

Surrendering the Secret
By: Pat Layton
www.surrenderingthesecret.com

Additional Reading:

The following are available through amazon.com

Forbidden Grief: The Unspoken Pain of Abortion
By: Theresa Burke

Her Choice to Heal
By: Sydna Masse
Available at www.amazon.com

I'll Hold You in Heaven
By: Jack Hayford

Fatherhood Aborted
By: Guy Condon and David Hazard

Redeeming a Father's Heart
By: Kevin Burke, LSW, David Wemhoff & Marvin Stockwell

Video:

Beyond Regret: Entering Into Healing and Wholeness After Abortion
Available at www.amazon.com

NOTES

NOTES

NOTES

NOTES

NOTES

NOTES

Made in the USA
Columbia, SC
06 March 2021